RIPE STRAWBERRIES ARE SWEETER

Why I'm Waiting Instead of Dating

SAVANNA SHELDEN

WESTBOW
PRESS®
A DIVISION OF THOMAS NELSON
& ZONDERVAN

Scripture taken from the King James Version of the Bible.

Scripture taken from the New King James Version®. Copyright ©
1982 by Thomas Nelson. Used by permission. All rights reserved.

Scripture quotations taken from the Amplified® Bible (AMP),
Copyright © 2015 by The Lockman Foundation Used by permission

WestBow Press books may be ordered through booksellers or by contacting:

WestBow Press
A Division of Thomas Nelson & Zondervan
1663 Liberty Drive
Bloomington, IN 47403
www.westbowpress.com
1 (866) 928-1240

ISBN: 978-1-9736-1232-2 (sc)
ISBN: 978-1-9736-1231-5 (e)

Library of Congress Control Number: 2017919643

Print information available on the last page.

WestBow Press rev. date: 01/19/2018

For all those in search of something
better than 'normal.'

Contents

Acknowledgements

Jesus, Lover of my soul: You've led me to the altar of Calvary and vowed to be far more than a human could ever promise. I wish I could say 'forever and always,' and mean it in the same sense that You do, but the only thing I can pledge with confidence is, 'I'll always need You.'

Mom, your counsel and prayers have saved my soul and my future from ruin countless times. Thank you for yielding yourself as a living canvas for God to illustrate the color of true love on. I realize that my understanding of Him has your character as its foundation. No doubt, a child's first Bible, rather than being a cute edition filled with pictures, is their mother. Thank you for making us—your children—your priority mission field.

Friends and family, you've already learned one of the most essential lessons of this book: How to wait. You are great encouragers and motivators—I didn't have the heart to face you yet another time without having finished "The Strawberry Story."

Once again, thank you, Kevin. You've lived up to your reputation as "the answer man." It's safe to answer your phone now. We probably just want to say 'Hi.'

A Word to My Readers

To write this book has been the work of a few short years, but to live up to the standard it contains will be the work of my life. I don't 'have it all figured out.' But I find a daily supply of transforming power in the One who is "holy, harmless, undefiled, separate from sinners," yet somehow, "not ashamed to call them brethren" (Hebrews 7:26, 2:11 NKJV).

The same Savior Who has gotten my attention and captured my heart, washed me from my sins in His own life-blood, and helped me set my sails toward true fulfillment, is calling you. Are you willing to start the voyage to a better harbor? The sea that looks so intimidating is really waves of mercy.

Introduction

"Doubtless, God could have made a better berry,
but doubtless, God never did."
– Dr. William Butler, 17th-century English writer

Strawberries. The world's favorite berry? Yep. The whopping 4,594,539 tons grown on Planet Earth annually (not including China's estimated 2,100,000 tons) weigh enough to crush any doubt. California's one billion *pounds* (not tons) alone are enough to circle the globe 15 times if each strawberry was laid berry to berry.[1] From the days a small ancestor of today's berry was gathered wild from the woods, impaled on pieces of straw ('straw' berries) and sold in English villages, to the present, we've never stopped being in love.

My family and I are no exception—we relish strawberries as much as most everyone else. As lifelong Alaskans, however, we have a hard time getting an edible, abundant supply of them. While our truckers do their

---

[1] Strawberry facts gleaned from Wikipedia & <u>imp.missouri.edu</u>.

best, transporting fresh food to "the edge of the known universe"[2] is an undertaking that has its good and bad days. Again and again, what we wish could be breakfast looks more like candidates for "Moldy" Mary's shopping basket ("Moldy" Mary was a woman hired to purchase the decaying fruit used in the discovery of penicillin). "Oh well. At least we have dried fruit," we tell ourselves as we push our cart elsewhere, feeling like stranded explorers forced to exist on hard-tack biscuits.

Our shopping attitude has undergone a change in the past couple of years, though. Lately, we're making it through the produce aisle without so much as even a second glance or a moan. The 'rotten' deal of far-north shopping has been rendered bearable by a cheering realization: With the aid of high tunnel greenhouses, we can grow berries that are bigger than the biggest and sweeter than the sweetest! And, if we boycott 'strawberries-only' meals and actually store some up, they can be enjoyed throughout the fruit-famine days of winter. "Farewell, store-bought!"

As fledgling strawberry farmers, each day holds new lessons for us. The why and how of production gives us plenty of food for thought, but the richest experience of all is learning awe-inspiring spiritual truths from our Creator. Today, many people view agriculture (gardening/farming) as merely a nice hobby for those who 'happened'

---

[2] A term coined by a non-Alaskan business agent trying to justify exorbitant shipping rates. We get a real kick out of it!

to get green thumbs, a livelihood for commercial farmers, and a source of groceries for everyone else—unaware that God had something deeper in mind when He made it an aspect of life on Earth. Just like He walked with Adam and Eve in the Garden of Eden, He waits to meet each of us in the garden. He calls us away from what's artificial and shallow, to the simplicity and beauty of nature. He asks us to do something our peace-less culture and our peace-less hearts have taught us to avoid like the plague: To face quietness, and in so doing, to face Him (see Psalm 46:10). He has revolutionary concepts to teach us. He wants to help us grasp the mysteries of His Word through the easily-seen things He has created. As we come to understand and live by the principles of His kingdom, the damage sin has done in our hearts is healed, and a bright horizon of love, obedience, and joy opens up before us.

This book is a compilation of the truths about dating, relationships, and true love that God has shown my family and me, first in His Word, and second, in His world … through strawberries. His grace, dripping with compassion and glowing with hope, has reached us where we are, and knowing that His gifts aren't for hoarding, I pray these words will be a means of passing that grace on, reaching you where you are. May you be touched by the love of the One Who is so intimately involved in His creation that He cares to whisper His thoughts to this speck of a world.

1

Guardian of the Garden

"She realized that His eyes were searching
into the very depths of her heart
and knew all that was there far better than she did herself."
– From Hannah Hurnard's allegory,
Hind's Feet on High Places

Last summer, our strawberries really took a hard hit from rodents, wasps, and slugs. We'd admire a beauty and say, "One more day, and it'll be ripe enough," only to discover the next day that Mrs. Vole (similar to a mouse) shared our opinion, but got up earlier. Or, we'd go to pick another one and be startled to discover it hollow as a balloon and the hideout of a belligerent wasp. We like playing freeze-tag, but not 'sting-tag.' On one such occasion, I could only hope that my hay-farming brother's arriving customers wouldn't doubt my sanity as I raced around the yard, apparently feeling quite energetic on this sunny morn!

As we brainstormed for a way to cut down on our losses, increasing casualties caused our frustration to build: "If only the critters would just eat a whole berry, but they insist on taking one or two bites out of each one!" Our hopes of bringing each juicy jewel to ripened perfection began to droop. Would we be back to dried fruit, despite hundreds of vibrant, fruit-laden strawberry plants?

One afternoon, after viewing yet another exhibit of the pests' handiwork, I started picking strawberries that were just a little unripe. My reasoning was, 'Better early than never.' The fruit wouldn't be the greatest thing we ever tasted, but at least it was something. As I filled my container, the Lord filled my mind with thought. He said, "You know, you're picking those because of fear." I agreed with Him—I was acting out of desperation. He then drew my attention to a profound and convicting parallel: We do the same thing in the area of love and relationships. As humans (and especially youth), we long to find and 'pick' that person like no other, that 'strawberry' that will fill life with blissful sweetness. But, unwilling to wait on God's timing and plans for our lives, we often justify thoughts and actions that are a sad compromise, just like I talked myself into picking those unripe strawberries. This compromise mentality is known to thrive in the modern 'I want it now' dating game, hence this book's sub-title. Like my Heavenly Father pointed out, our unwillingness to wait is rooted in fear: Fear of being 'ancient' on our wedding day ('overripe'), fear of never marrying at all (equivalent to many with rotting and going to waste), fear of losing 'the one' to competitors (the 'voles', 'slugs', and 'wasps' of life), or of just plain fainting from hunger before "the time appointed" finally arrives. And, short-changed by that fear, our relationships end up falling short of all we hoped for. After all, prematurely-picked strawberries don't hold a candle to ones that have taken their time ripening on the plant.

We are under no obligation to live under the power of fear: This domineering emotion that pushes us to fall for the sub-standard and keeps us from tasting the best. God has presented us with a replacement. It's called 'trust.' It used to be on our money, and it's one of the most common words a person will ever hear in church, but if you're like me, you might be wondering what it actually comes down to. I like things to be practical, to know what to do with what I hear. That's why I love the definition of trust a dear friend of mine (AKA Mom) read to me the other day:

> *"Confidence; a reliance or resting of the mind on the integrity, veracity (habitual truthfulness), justice, friendship or other sound principle of another person."*
> – *Noah Webster's 1828 Dictionary*

"Another person" … Someone to trust in … The missing factor in this mix of strawberry, pests, and expectant/ exasperated farmer—the solution we have yet to come up with in our greenhouse, but that already exists for each love-seeking heart: Protection for the ripening 'strawberry,'

3

so we no longer have to fear. In all probability, the answer for our greenhouse will not comprise of packing lunches for my younger brother so he can watch day and night with all the vigilance of the President's bodyguard. But the God Who has set His love upon us has pledged His own constant Presence as the Protector of our dreams. He invites us to trust Him, to put the 'strawberry' in His capable hands.

'But,' our hearts are so prone to whimper, 'I don't know if I'm ready to take such a radical step.' It feels like there's some kind of risk involved, a possibility that life could turn out bizarre, restricted, or miserable if we dare to relinquish control. The summer I was seven, my mom frequently took my siblings and me to play at a lake. Our family was clearing land for our new house nearby, and the invigorating water was something to look forward to all day (as the adults worked and we children jumped up and down on brush piles). While I enjoyed the man-made sandy beach (that's desperate Alaskans for you), the inflatable floaties, and the picnic, the diving board was outside my comfort zone. After watching various members of my family gleefully catapult themselves into the depths, I decided to give it a try. I made my way across the dock until at last, I stood on the very end of 'the plank.' And I stood there. And I stood there some more, trying and trying to 'get up my courage.' I still remember the feeling—the paralyzing indecision. When I finally jumped, it dawned on me that my own thoughts were the most traumatic part of the whole thing.

I'm still the same little girl inside. Time after time, I find myself only a jump away from complete trust and surrender, torn between the life of faith I know I want to live, and what's natural and feels safe. And I stand there. And I stand there some more. But this time, it's not a freak surge of bravery that makes me jump into the unknown. The Word of God says, "The love of Christ constraineth us" (2 Corinthians 5:14 KJV), or urges us with an irresistible power. Unless we refuse to 'let it get to us,' it disarms our every prejudice and breaks down our every defense. That's what the definition of trust I quoted earlier points to: Trust springs from a knowledge of someone's character; it's the byproduct of a loving friendship. If it's hard for us to trust God, we don't know Him like we should. My 'trust-o-meter' reads highest as I absorb the Bible and personally experience Him. I become more and more sure that He has the most trust-worthy character I have ever seen. In His faithfulness, His mercy, His forgiveness, and every other quality, I have grounds for a "resting of the mind." I have no doubt that in all He has done, is doing, or ever will do, His only motive is selfless love. The physical and emotional agony He put Himself through on the Cross make it evident that His goal is not to deprive me of good opportunities, but instead, to save me from evil and its painful consequences. Those nail-wounded hands are the safest place I could ever hope for in which to put my life.

While one look at His great sacrifice overwhelmingly earns my trust, the small things He does for me nurture it in a special way. They make me aware of just how personal our relationship is—that the loving Savior of some 2,000 years ago is the Man in my life today. I'm encouraged that if He cares about my tiniest wants or needs, He hasn't forgotten about my greater ones, and even when it seems like He has, it's only because He's taking the time to work out a deeper, more extensive blessing for me.

An example of this tender attention to small things took place as my sister and I set to work designing the cover of this book.[3] We knew that a picture of a perfectly ripe strawberry simply *must* grace it; nothing else would do. As we searched for the most photogenic berry in our patch, our eyes lit upon 'The One.' Large, perfect, and … heart-shaped. What more could we ask for? Ripeness. It was days away from being ready. Maybe even a week. Hmmm … how to keep it safe? Visions of rodent-proof cages, 'Do not touch' signs for two-legged strawberry predators, etc., sent our engineering wheels into orbit. But before we got too elaborate, they screeched to a halt with the thought, "If this whole book is about the ability of God to keep things safe until they ripen, why not ask Him to do it now in this little thing?" We did. We prayed and left it there, right in the middle of *Varmint Main Street*. Day after day it sat there, untouched and untouchable. It ripened to the highest degree of strawberry excellence, with not even one tiny bug-bite to mar its perfection.

---

[3] The West Bow Press design team did a great job finishing it up for us.

With hearts full of gratitude and awe, we snapped the photo we'd envisioned (you can see it on the front cover of this book).

I have no doubt that there was something more than chance involved in the ripening of that strawberry. There's no way the pests just happened to miss it. It was right in the open, and the berries all around it were ruined. The Guardian of the Garden heard our prayer and intervened. He was just waiting to be trusted …

"The Rest of the Story": Introduction to Chapters 2-9

"In these lessons direct from nature,
there is a simplicity and purity
that makes them of the highest value."
– Christ's Object Lessons, p. 24

I'm so thankful the Lord rescued my family from the venomous jaws of the TV. "Worthless things" (Psalm 119:37 NKJV) and worse-than-worthless things no longer hemorrhage into our home, and in place of watching other people live life, we've gotten a life. We work. We make things. We play. We read. We think. And we talk ... We have conversations about deep things, things that really matter. One comment is apt to turn into a feast of discussion as each person brings their unique perspective to the 'table.' It reminds me of the ancient Greek philosophers who sat together and dissected life, only, we've invited a Guest to be with us that many of them didn't know: "The Spirit of truth" (John 14:16, 17 KJV).

While God gave the strawberry lesson in Chapter 1 when I was alone, almost all the lessons in the chapters ahead were unearthed during these 'feasts of discussion.' When

I shared my greenhouse revelation with my family at worship time one day, they responded with characteristic enthusiasm and heavenly inspiration. Almost everyone had a new thought to add, until lesson after lesson had surfaced, and we realized just how much there is to learn from the lowly strawberry! The comments of insightful friends, more days in the greenhouse, and some online research added the finishing touches. As you read, I think you'll be amazed at how perfect the berry/love parallels are!

2

Grow Your Roots Before Your Fruits

"May you be rooted deep in love ... that you may really come to know ... through experience for yourselves, the love of Christ."
– Ephesians 3:17, 19 AMP

I can identify with the children of past generations who bored holes with their longing eyes into the pages of the Montgomery Ward and other mail-order catalogs. Starting in about February every year (I guess that must be spring in some places), a deluge of seed and plant-nursery catalogs comes in the mail, and we spend many a day drooling over all the things we want to grow. The corresponding deluge of packages that comes in the following months reveals that we don't do an exorbitant amount of narrowing down when placing our orders (we consider nearly all things agriculture a worthy investment).

There is an area we aren't so free in, however, and that is fruit trees. Plums, peaches, apricots, and other delights that promise they aren't afraid of 50 degrees below-zero are quite tempting, but we try not to be too gullible. Along with more than one ailing sapling, much of our faith in such claims has been uprooted. After letting page after page of mouth-watering pictures and descriptions rub in the cons of our climate, we settle on something more realistic … like strawberries. And I have to say, when they start producing, our peach cravings hit zero rpm's, so, all playing aside, we really are thankful.

Once my mom has looked through a company's paper catalog, she likes to go to their website and place her order: One click. That'll be 100 strawberry plants. "Oh, this one looks good." Click. One hundred more. "Oh, I forgot, so and so told me this one did well for them." Click click. Two hundred more … Cart contents: 600 bare root strawberry plants. Moment of shock … Proceed to Checkout … Keep in mind this takes place mid-winter. Then, come spring, when her daring online purchases have become only a distant memory, FedEx arrives with our card-board-encased destiny, at least for a couple of weeks. Forget to-do lists and agendas; it's time to plant strawberries! All of them. Six hundred is nothing for a commercial operation, but it feels like a lot to home gardeners still transitioning to that side. Our purchasing agent mutters doubts about her own sanity, but we get an efficient planting method down, and before too long, the rooty masses have been soaked, trimmed, and tucked into their greenhouse beds. Leaves soon appear, followed by flowers, all within a short time of receiving them as a peculiar package.

As much as we don't like to, we pinch off all or nearly all the flowers these new arrivals make in their first year. It's not healthy for them to be bearing fruit during that time. They only have so much energy, and as new plants, that energy needs to go into establishing a vigorous root-system, rather than into producing berries. For commercial reasons, some farmers plant, harvest from, then uproot their strawberries every season, and in that case, the pinching step is obviously bypassed, but for growers who want their plants to survive the winter, it's a sensible practice. The time spent on roots will also be well-repaid in future quality and quantity of fruit. We learned a little saying that makes this principle easy to remember: "Little roots, little fruits."

Love Lesson:

If we want our lives to amount to more than an uprooted heap of shallow, short-lived pleasures 'when it's all said and done,' if we want to have families that will stand a chance of surviving the hard times—of holding on until the sun shines again, we'd better start pinching off flowers. Not every impulse we have should be allowed to bloom and produce something. Just as it'd be easy to think that little strawberry flowers wouldn't affect something so huge as the whole plant's survival, we may downplay the importance of guarding our affections, but King Solomon, a man who learned the hard way, warns us, "Keep and guard your heart with all vigilance and above all that you guard, for out of it flow the springs of life" (Proverbs 4:23 AMP). In other words, every single aspect of our lives will be affected by the direction we let our hearts go.

As new 'plants'—as youth—we have something more important to focus on than 'strawberries.' Becoming established—getting to the point where we're growing well in all aspects, but especially spiritually—is what demands our attention. God has a purpose for each of us to pour ourselves into, a calling to take hold of, separate from if we get married or not. We have to become secure and fulfilled in pursuing that, not pining away for what we think is the missing puzzle piece in life. It doesn't make sense mathematically, but with relationships, 1 + 1 = 1. We can't expect to be half a person, find our 'other half,' and be one-fleshed happily-ever-after. If we aren't happy and content alone, we will be unhappy and discontent together, and if we have children, we will simply be multiplying the victims of our bad characters. In my short life, I've already had ample opportunity to see this played out. Eyes that at first were filled with stars become eyes filled with tears. Dreams turn into nightmares, and homes that were supposed to be fortresses of faithful love sink into ashes that only the mercy of God can bring beauty from.

'Complete in Christ' (see Colossians 2:10) is to be the name of the first chapter in every love story. We each have to come to the point where we embrace that God is and has everything we need; that the love of Jesus is the only love that can satisfy our hearts' deepest longings. And when we've been satisfied by that love—transformed from love black-holes into love fountains—He just might give us someone to share our abundance with. Actually, He has already given us the whole world to share it with, but you know what I'm referring to. The sacrifice we've made to keep our focus on the roots of commitment to God will then be seen in the sweet, abundant 'strawberries' of loving marriages and families.

I'm going to close this chapter with two quotes from one of my favorite authors, Ellen White. If the counsel given in them were loved and followed, how many empty hearts could be filled, before they were filled with something that broke them!

> *"Many who are seeking for happiness will be disappointed in their hopes, because they seek it amiss. True happiness is not to be found in selfish gratification, but in the path of duty. God desires man to be happy, and for this reason He gave him the precepts of His law, that in obeying these he might have joy at home and abroad. While he stands in his moral integrity, true to principle, having the control of all his powers, he cannot be*

miserable. With its tendrils entwined about God, the soul will flourish amid unbelief and depravity. But many who are constantly looking forward for happiness fail to receive it, because, by neglecting to discharge the little duties and observe the little courtesies of life, they violate the principles upon which happiness depends."

– Our High Calling, p. 63

"Human love can never bear its precious fruit until it is united with the divine nature and trained to grow heavenward."

– In Heavenly Places, p. 202

Strawberry Cravings

I trust God to hold you until the time,
In purity's beauty, you will be mine.
Separate, in Christ, we'll have been made complete,
And together in Him, our love will be sweet…

I trust God to hold you until the time…
Meanwhile, 'round Jesus my tendrils entwine,
Trained by His Spirit to grow heavenward,
For His nature alone can make human love pure.

– Savanna Shelden

3

"Make Haste Slowly"

"O Lord, I am a fool ... Leave me
not to my own blindness ..."
– John Bunyan, author of the classic, Pilgrim's Progress

On many a June morning, breakfast comes to a standstill with the animated announcement (usually from Mom): "You guys, I forgot—there's strawberries!", and we mobilize like firemen to go pick. Sometimes, when production is still picking up and only some are ripe, one person gets selected for 'strawberry duty.' With all the ceremony used to crown a king, the returning harvester marches in and deposits the container on the counter, amid the "oohing" and "aahing" of all.

I won't say any names (I don't want to over-use my younger brother), but there are some of our number who have needed their picking skills, ahem, fine-tuned. After the initial triumphal march, at times a look at the fruit has given occasion for yet another exposition from Mom on the meaning of "*daaark* red." A factor in the blunder can be looking at a berry's sun-kissed side alone (the part with the most color) and deciding it's ripe enough, only to realize too late that the whitish-pink underside still leaves much to be desired. Nonetheless, no matter the reason, a picked strawberry is picked, so we eat the present and hope for the future.

Love Lesson:

None of us have the necessary skills to pick the perfect life companion, or even in the case of the right one, to know when. The problem is, we only get one chance. The only second chances approved of by the Word of God are if one's spouse has been unfaithful or died (see Matthew 19:9 & 1 Corinthians 7:39). "'Til death do us part" was meant to be more than just nice-sounding words—to last longer than the bride's bouquet. Just like with strawberries, we can't glue or tape our poor selections back to the stem. We're stuck. We'll have to 'eat' the present and hope for the future, a future that is now dependent on someone else's choices as well as our own. We can't afford to be 'in the dark' on the definition of "*daaark* red." Often, attraction causes us to look at only certain aspects of a person's character and decide they're 'ripe' enough. Are we only focusing on where the sun has shined: Their strengths and good qualities? Are we blind to, or excusing, traits that are unacceptable? From what

I've seen, it's the very thing people excuse before they're married that becomes the bitterest part of being married.

We have to be sure the person we marry is the person we want to have to love. I know that sounds very cold and unromantic, but it's true. We like to think of love as a passionate feeling, but many times, it's most powerfully conveyed the moment we choose to go against our feelings. When we commit to love someone forever, we're pre-determining what choice we'll make every minute of every day, no matter the choices they do or don't make. In highlighting choice, I'm not ruling feelings out of the marriage equation—they certainly have their place, but when a man gets home from work, for example, and the baby is sick, his wife is moody and needs a shower, the 3-year-old has clogged the toilet, and the sink is full of dishes that apparently weren't used to make dinner, *feelings* aren't what holds the family together. They tend to do a disappearing act when life gets real. But it is then that love, true love, so well described in 1 Corinthians 13 (the Bible's 'love chapter'), is in its element.

How can we know for sure if we've found true, ripe love or not? Just as my mom patiently instructs her novice strawberry-harvesters, God desires to help us overcome our hasty childishness and learn what ripeness should look like. He urges us to submit ourselves to His flawless discernment: "Trust in the Lord with all thine heart; and lean not unto thine own understanding. In all thy ways acknowledge him, and he shall direct thy paths."

(Proverbs 3:5, 6 KJV). We simply don't know what's best or what would make us happy. Our finite minds reach out after small things—we are in need of the Mind that seeks greater things for us than we are wise or mature enough to seek for ourselves. I really see the truth of this when I look back at all the things I've thought I wanted over the years—desires that were never granted. A mixture of shudders and praises well up inside me as I see all that my Father's loving intervention has spared me from. There is only one Heart with my best good in mind, and it's not mine, for sure. Unless I'm under the direct influence of the grace of God, an alternate spelling for my name is F–O–O–L, and I sign all my grandest life-plans with it, big and bold like John Hancock (the first signer of the Declaration of Independence). But, merciful, ever merciful, my Shepherd waits to carry me home when those plans have turned into nightmares and bondage and heal the wounds I've inflicted on myself. Then He tells me, with love so unshakeable it's bewildering, that He still has plans for me—the ones He's been promising all along …

'Berry-picking' Pointers:

> *"Keep your eyes wide open before marriage*
> *and half-shut thereafter."*
> *– Benjamin Franklin*

While my family and I believe that if God calls a person to be single, to run from this relationship status is hazardous, we frequently talk about what qualities to look for in a potential spouse, should God ever lead us that way. It's good to develop solid principles and high standards ahead of time. That way, as the attractions, distractions, and decisions of life come upon us, we'll be clear on what we believe and what to do. In my family's conversations, instead of some long shopping list, two main ingredients always come to the forefront:

- Unmistakable conversion
- Utter humility

Without them, no home will ever be a place of love, joy, and peace. But they are so exotic they can't be found just anywhere, or cheaply purchased. They bear the stamp of a far country, yes, Heaven itself. A person could look the whole world over, but only one place carries them. That place is the Cross of Jesus. There, where He drank the bitterness of your sin and my sin (the breaking of His 10-commandment law), the power to live like we've never lived before flows in sweet abundance.

Let's get into these two prerequisites a little. While they won't be the only characteristics that should eventually be considered, anyone without them should never be 'in the running.' And, as a matter of fact, anyone without them should never be 'in the looking.' The best way to get something is to become it first, because we attract what we are. I guess looking within should cure us all of 'shopping.' How many of us can say that we've been 'unmistakably converted,' and even if we can, what about 'utterly humble'? If we're confident that that label fits us, we must be proud of our humility. I don't know about you, but thinking about these matters makes me feel like my wedding day is far away indeed. If God ever sees fit to surprise me with the knowledge that I'm ready to take that step, I'll know it's yet another one of His undeserved favors.

Happy Relationship Ingredient #1: Unmistakable Conversion:

How can we know? " ... By their fruits ye shall know them" (Matthew 7:20 KJV). What is fruit? Actions ... And better yet, *re*actions. But, even a particle of attraction is likely to unfit us for the job of Fruit Inspector. We're apt to completely gloss over the bad, and blow what good may exist (in reality or our imaginations) to such proportions that we fail to see the snare we're about to step into. Our only safety is to pray like we've never prayed before, and realize our need of wise counsel. People 'in love' tend to make their board of directors 'me, myself, and I' (i.e. 'What do you think of her?' 'Amazing!' 'What do you think of her?' 'She's wonderful!' 'And what do you think of her?' 'You should marry her. If you don't, I'm going to,'), when, instead, they need to admit that their judgment is likely not in full working order. While we can't heed the counsel of every person who walks by, we should highly esteem, humbly seek, and prayerfully consider the discernment of those who've shown themselves to be firmly rooted in the truth of God's Word. It's common to expect God to answer our prayers for wisdom with some kind of amazing revelation while we're on our knees, but His favorite method is to use other people. In place of goosebumps, we may get truths that are hard to hear, but if we pray for soft hearts, He'll give us far more than just the answer we need at the time: He'll make us so humble that we'll listen to His voice no matter where it comes from.

As we look for evidence of unmistakable conversion in someone, there's something else, in addition to Christ-centered counsel, that we can't afford to do without: TIME. Maybe the saying, 'Time heals all things' should be replaced with the more accurate, 'Time *reveals* all things.' The clock's busy hands have dug up many secrets. Being in a hurry is the best way to make mistakes, and disastrous ones at that—everyone knows that high-speed collisions are the worst. A false front can only last so long. We have to give people time to show their true colors, and in more realistic settings than candle-light dinners and concerts.

How much time should we allow? The love stories God writes for His children are as unique as our fingerprints, so I'm not making a doctrine out of this, but I believe it's prudent to get to know a person for one to two years before pursuing anything closer than the foundational 'brothers and sisters in Christ' relationship. My family's personal experience has shown that by then, the newness of friendship has worn off, and patterns and tendencies in character have become apparent. We've known people who were newly baptized, eagerly studying the Bible, and sharing heartfelt testimonies every week in church, people who wanted to come to our house every day because they loved us so much, flip into people whose life-mission seems to be spreading false accusations, people who are suicidal and in mental hospitals, people who are so full of hate and anger that their faces are frightening to look at, all in a couple of years' time. In view of a lifetime, what's the hurry? As I once heard it said, "It would be better to spend 30 years with the right person than 50 years with the wrong person."

"Tarry, tarry, tarry, tarry, think again before you marry."
– Charles H. Spurgeon, 19th-century English preacher

Learn from the Susu and Avoid the 'So-So' (or Worse):

The Susu people of Western Africa have a custom that makes use of the principles we've been discussing in this section (seeking counsel and allowing time):

When a young man meets a girl he's interested in, he has to go to her parents with one of his relatives, such as an uncle. The uncle is the spokesperson, probably to the relief of the young man (who is likely to say something 'memorable' in this moment when impressions are of the essence). Once the uncle has made his nephew's intentions known, the parents ask for time, usually two weeks, so they can discuss the idea with their daughter. During this period, they investigate the young man's character and reputation. After gathering enough information, they make a decision and get back to the young man. If they give him the go-ahead, a relationship starts. If not, a disappointed young man must look elsewhere for his bride.

Okay, time to talk about the second qualification that comes up in my family's relationship powwows:

Happy Relationship Ingredient #2: Utter Humility:

I'm going to empty part of the thesaurus on this one: Humility is central. Critical. Crucial. Fundamental. Imperative. Indispensable. Key. Vital. Even the most unmistakably converted person will still have flaws, but we need to ask, What is he/she doing about these flaws? Is this person growing in grace, or growing worse? When they stand face to face with their sins, what's their reaction: Pride, or humility? If we see that pride is on the throne, we should turn and run. Pride is every bit as intoxicating as alcohol, and can extinguish love as fast as my grandma's old-fashioned candle snuffer. Pride is a peace-repellent, for "only by pride cometh contention" (Proverbs 13:10 KJV). It threw even Heaven itself into a state of war, and we can't expect anything less from it here on Earth. Pride lives under an illusion of perfection that no one else seems to see. Its greatest fear is looking bad, but the only thing it ever succeeds in is just that: Looking bad. Humility, on the other hand, makes us admirable in the midst of our worst failures and imperfections. It doesn't excuse or cling to them. It doesn't blame them on someone else. It lays things out how they are so they don't have to stay that way. It values a Christ-like character more than its own feelings and opinions. It makes it possible for wounded love to regenerate.

Humility is the fruit of unmistakable conversion, but in so many hearts who claim to have surrendered all to Jesus, it is nowhere to be found. May God reveal to us our pride, and, in light of its ugliness, our need to be converted "daily" (Luke 9:23 KJV). If you don't think you have an issue with pride, read the following insight, and join me in going to "the throne of grace, that we may obtain mercy and find grace to help in time of need" (Hebrews 4:16 KJV):

> *"Humility is perfect quietness of heart. It is not for me to be fretful or upset or irritated or annoyed or disappointed. It is to expect nothing, to be surprised at nothing that is done to me, to feel no hurt at anything done against me. It is to be at rest when nobody praises me or when I am blamed or despised. It is to have a blessed peace in the Lord*

where I can go in and shut the door and kneel to my Father in secret with a deep sea of calmness when all around is trouble. It is the fruit of the Lord Jesus Christ's work on Calvary's cross. It is seen in the lives of His own: those who offer Him their absolute surrender and who follow the leading of His Holy Spirit."

– Andrew Murray, 19th-century South African pastor/missionary

Lord, take me down the road, no matter how painful it is, that brings me to this place!

4

Patiently Preoccupied

"Don't chase your dreams. Chase the Lord!"
– Charles H. Spurgeon

Chances are, you've heard the saying, 'A watched pot never boils.' For your information, the stovetop and the garden have something in common: Watched fruit 'never' ripens. If our strawberries are green, we ignore whatever longings we may have for them and go our way, focusing on all else that demands our attention (which is a lot—try farming!). Unless we want to make ourselves miserably bored and worthless, we have no other choice. Plus, there's a lot more to an Alaskan summer than just strawberries. We'd miss many other pleasures if we sat there staring at them all day.

Love Lesson:

You might chuckle at how basic the paragraph you just read is, but what it symbolizes is so serious and relevant that it really struck me. Always keeping our dreams for the future in the forefront of our minds makes us worthless and miserable in the present. We neglect what we're supposed to be doing, and our characters start to look like our tomato patch last summer: An absolute JUNGLE (though it didn't get that way because I was gazing at green strawberries). We lose the ability to appreciate all the blessings we already have, because all we can think about is what we don't have.

It's as if we believe that unless we make our desires our supreme focus, we can't possibly get them. On the contrary, God remembers the desires of those who forget their own in the pursuit of His. He delights in being the diligent Care-taker of all that they have buried under heap after heap of unselfishness. His promise to them is, "Delight thyself also in the Lord; and he shall give thee the desires of thine heart" (Psalm 37:4 KJV). He can say this with confidence, for in becoming people who find their delight in Him, they've become safe to gratify.

The following love story beautifully illustrates the points I've been making. Ever since we heard it on a missionary story DVD[4], we've been telling and retelling it. It's refreshing in a world where the majority views life through self-interest-tinted (or shall I say, *tainted*) glasses:

Dwayne, a young American, prepared to go to the Philippines as a missionary helicopter pilot. Being single, he got teased, "You'll find someone over there." He felt quite confident that no such thing would happen, unless she was some missionary doctor or nurse—a far-fetched idea in his mind. In his own words, he was "not interested in females," and went unattached and planning to stay that way. He threw himself into the work he went there to do, and, becoming acquainted with the weed-whacker-like aircraft he was to pilot, had met his 'other half' for the time being. His skill proved to be an immense relief to the mission clinic, as the staff would no longer be wearied with attending to their scattered patients on foot. Whether the need was administering medicine in the villages or transporting those in critical condition to the clinic, the helicopter fit into the project like hand in glove.

Wendy, an unmarried young American, was working in a certain clinic in the Philippines as a missionary nurse. Raised in a missionary family, she felt it was a dream come true. The need was great, and the locals gratefully acknowledged that the medical missionary work was bringing them a new life. When a helicopter pilot named

---

[4] "Having Nothing, Having It All" by David Gates/Gospel Ministries International

Dwayne joined the team, she and the other staff could help so many more people, and they were glad to not have to hike anymore.

(Big grin ...)

As time went on, and Dwayne spent more time with Wendy, his tune started to change. The idea of "finding someone over there" wasn't sounding so far-fetched after all. And, just like he'd thought, she was a missionary nurse. Their only difficulty was finding time to grow their relationship—a challenge in that cultural setting. Wendy left it in the Lord's hands with the words, "If this is from You, You'll work it out." The necessary helicopter arrangement of pilot + nurse turned out to be the direct provision of their loving Father, and Dwayne and Wendy had the time they needed as they flew from place to place. Wendy kept praying, "Is this Your will? Is this from You?" as their relationship progressed, but Dwayne had no doubts from the beginning. It became clear to Wendy, though, as she got to know Dwayne better, that he was who he appeared to be; she knew God was bringing the man for her into her life.

As a married couple, they find that "the nurse/pilot combo is great." Right when many people are getting their first stomach-ache (heart-ache, more like) from the unripe 'strawberry' they've picked, Dwayne and Wendy are joyfully serving God together. With bright countenances, they testify that when we surrender to God's timing and focus on serving Him, life "works out far beyond our dreams and imaginations."

> *"The Lord is good unto them that wait for*
> *him, to the soul that seeketh him."*
> *— Lamentations 3:25 KJV*

5

DUI's: Dating Under
the Influence

*"Medieval stone masons carved strawberry designs on
altars and around the tops of pillars in churches and
cathedrals to symbolize perfection and righteousness."*
— University of Missouri

*Do perfection and righteousness come to mind
when others look at our relationships?*

The following views could be controversial, depending
on who you are, but please put yourself in our soil-kissed
shoes and try to understand: We give many tours of our
greenhouses all summer long, most of the time at the
request of our visitors. Even if they haven't come to buy
produce, we enjoy sharing the bounty God has given us,
and almost everyone leaves with a cucumber, zucchini,
or other surplus veggies. But ... (how should I say this?),

we appreciate having a choice in the gift-giving. Okay, I might as well be up-front: It's an exercise in meekness for us when people walk into our greenhouse, help themselves to our precious strawberries as if they were free finger food at some event, and we have to watch the fruit of our labors find lodging under belts that have no sweaty hours of work under them. To smile at our unruly (and did I mention, adult) guests with all the grace of accommodating hosts requires will-power. You may think we sound selfish, but Alaska is no Garden of Eden. We work hard for what we produce and feel that our garden is no different than our bank account, and that for someone to take from it without asking is stealing. But even the polite and proper don't seem to think that way. It's as if strawberries do something to people ...

We try to give our munching visitors the benefit of the doubt (i.e., "Maybe garden etiquette is different where they're from"), but there is talk of also giving them the benefit of a homemade sign. We hope some paint and whimsical poetry that conveys our protective feelings will have this awkward situation resolved before too long.

Love Lesson:

Around strawberries, many people act in surprising and uncharacteristic ways. So, if we're going to continue with our theme parallel, people must act in surprising and uncharacteristic ways when it comes to love and relationships. Consider this quote from a powerful book for youth entitled *Messages to Young People*:

> *"It is here that the youth show less intelligence than on any other subject; it is here that they refuse to be reasoned with. The question of marriage seems to have a bewitching power over them."(p. 447).*

Notice it reads we "show" less intelligence, not we 'have' less intelligence. This isn't about I.Q's; it's about what we choose to make use of or not. We aren't being faulted for being young and inexperienced. Really, there's nothing wrong with that. Youth were meant to go to the school of long talks (with their elders), so they wouldn't have to spend so much time in the school of hard knocks. Where the trouble lies is when we compound our problems by being young, inexperienced, *and* headstrong. You may think I'm harping on the need for humility and seeking counsel, but when the 'love-bug' hits, this is where so many of us go wrong. Even those who have gone right in every other area lose their heads and their desire to take anything seriously but their own ideas.

Does it make any sense that those who've loved and wanted the best for us all our lives would suddenly be intent on short-circuiting our happiness when it comes to romance? Sadly, we act like it, and live as if this was our creed: 'Only my heart, this fluttering, melting, dreaming thing, is fit to give an impartial, unbiased judgement' ('Order in the court! Order in the court! A piece of conclusive evidence that this relationship should go forward has surfaced: I've never been so in love before.' Famous last words ...). Are we ever 'under the influence'! And while we don't like to think of it, that influence is not simply our own feelings. It's a spell cast by the sinister mind whose greatest delight is tricking us into ruining our own happiness. How can we stay out from under this influence? By unswerving obedience to what God has said. Hanging our all on the Word of God makes us immune to deception. We don't have to be smart—we just have to be surrendered. God has given each of us our very own copy of *'Life for Dummies'* in the Bible. He says, *Turn away from the minefield of mirages you find in your own brain, those wrong thought processes that are so natural to you as a sinner. Turn to the unchanging truths of My Word—My thoughts written down—as your only source of reality. Nothing else is infallible. It is then, and only then, that you trust Me and I direct your paths—first and foremost, the pathways of your brain, and ultimately, the pathway of your life.*

The following poem is the result of some intensely convicting moments I've had with God—moments of 'sobering up,' of coming out from 'under the influence' and into alignment with truth. Accepting the fact that I must often disown my own feelings of 'love' if I want 'the real thing' has been like a bitter herb: Distasteful, but oh, so healing. I want nothing less than the love that I can still honestly say is love when the questions in this poem get through with it:

Can We Really Call It Love?

Love must be a slippery thing, because everywhere I go,
I hear of people falling in it—'dropping like flies', you know.
But before we simply smile, because love is crazy and blind,
Let's ask ourselves the questions that hang heavy on my mind:
Can we really call it 'love' when we hurt and destroy,
When we treat another's heart as if it is a toy?
Can we really call it 'love' when we give what is not our own,
To steal a heart's affections that belong to God alone?
Can we really call it 'love' when someone else's needs
Matter little to us, as long as what we want succeeds?
Can we really call it 'love' when attention is all we crave,
And we lose the holy focus that there are souls to save?
Can we really call it 'love' when our brazen only goal
Is to be a stumbling-block to a battling soul?
Can we really call it 'love' when it makes us vain and proud,
When it brings to our conscience a dark and heavy cloud?
Can we really call it 'love' when we give-in to compromise,
When principle is over-ruled by the sight of the eyes?
Can we really call it 'love' when it breaks down modesty,
And leaves good men in disgust at our indecency?
Can we really call it 'love' when on purity we trample,
When, for those who look up to us, we leave a poor example?
Can we really call it 'love,' when it's so cheap and disposable,
We'll give it away to anyone, and throw it away when we're full?
Can we really call it 'love,' when love has had no time to grow,
When 'the one' is a person we hardly even know?
Can we really call it 'love,' when it's gone in a flash,
When we treat our ex-idol like nothing more than trash?
Can we really call it 'love' when we leave behind the trails
Of a changing feeling that always fades and fails?

Savanna Shelden

Can we really call it 'love' when the ones we owe the most
Starve for our attention, while we are engrossed
In the thrills of fleeting passion, and the happy home we plan to make,
As if character can be transformed by dresses, suits, and cake?
Can we really call it 'love,' when it leaves us dissatisfied,
When, even though we're full of it, we're empty still inside?
Can we really call it 'love' when it holds us back
From tasting that Jesus can supply all that we lack?
Can we really call it 'love,' when, to believe its claims,
We must distrust Love Himself, and cast aside noble aims?
Can we really call it 'love' when it makes us hesitate
To ask for God's blessing, and run swiftly to our fate?
Can we really call it 'love,' when broken hearts are its main fruits,
When impatience and envy are its chiefest attributes?
Can we really call it 'love' when it makes us insincere,
When it takes away our vision, and makes our path unclear?
Can we really call it 'love' when it makes us stop our ears
To a friend's insight and counsel, and ignore a mother's tears?
Can we really call it 'love,' when we have to close our eyes
To the revealed will of God, and turn to the serpent's lies?
Can we really call it 'love,' when with duty it interferes,
When, in its dazzling darkness, love for Jesus disappears?
Can we really call it 'love,' when to obey its call,
Truth, right, and honor must to the wayside fall?
Can we really call it 'love,' when it's carnal and low,
When it's natural to a sinner, when it 'goes with the flow'?
Can we really call it 'love' when we write a tale of disgrace—
A record that, in the judgment, we will be ashamed to face?
Can we really call it 'love' when those who were friends must part,
When what could have been fellowship is a mess of guilty hearts?
Can we really call it 'love' when there are dark secrets to cover,
When children mourn over parents who no longer love each other?
Can we really call it 'love' when it has us go around
The law that is the only gate where love's true road is found?

Can we really call it 'love,' when it stands in enmity
To what the document named 'Christ' has published love to be?
Can we really call it 'love' when it has not a cent of love to its name,
When we see it's an imposter we have called this holy name?
Can we really call it 'love'? God forbid that we should.
With the light shining on it, I don't see how we could.
Will we cling to our feelings, and glory in our shame,
Or will we dare to call it by its rightful name?:
Enchanting evil spirit, Satan's bewitching spell,
A train that feels like Heaven, on the tracks to Hell;
An eye-catching trinket, but our souls are the price,
On an evil altar, a shameful sacrifice;
A mirage, an illusion, an alluring fraud,
In direct hostility to the ways of God;
A pit that only Mercy's arm can reach the bottom of,
And lift those who have fallen in what they thought was love,
And raise them to the atmosphere of love's pure, holy air,
And teach them they can only love if they are lifted there.

– Savanna Shelden

6

The Hidden Benefits of Being Hidden

"I'd have to say I pretty much did the complete opposite of waiting instead of dating. When I decided I wanted to get married, I went to the biggest strawberry patch I knew of, picked out the juiciest one I could find, and ran with it."

— A friend, in recounting his personal love story

Sometimes we have no clue a berry even exists, and are happily surprised at picking-time as we part the leaves and find a ruby-red jewel, all ready to delight us. On the other hand, some berries grow in such exposed places that they're always turning heads. However, experience has taught us that admiration can be costly, for it was an eye-catching strawberry that was snatched from her home by the fingers of a thief (visitors, you know). And, it was her attractive and hanging-in-plain-sight sister that was crushed against the side of the strawberry bed by a careless passerby.

Another insight we've gained is that the berry's location often determines what kind of person will pick it. Those who are bent on instant gratification grab the ones in the open, but diligent seekers peer among the glossy leaves until they're rewarded with sweet treasures that are beyond what they've imagined.

Love Lesson:

This one is split—half for the ladies, half for the gentlemen:

Ladies:

Just like my family and I take pleasure in our strawberries, we women long for someone to love and appreciate us. We crave attention from men because it feels good, and whether we get it through the way we look or the way we act, we usually succeed sooner or later. But is 'lust at first sight' equivalent with 'love at first sight'? What I'm saying is: We may get attention, but is it an attention worth wanting? Or should it be making our skin crawl and our legs run? When we dress in a way that shouts 'Look at my body!', we attract men who are slaves to their carnal natures. Wearing the 'leaves' of modesty will help us keep from being 'picked' by men who will steal our hearts to feed their own passions. It'll help us stay out of the way of those who are so self-centered that they don't think about the hearts their choices are breaking. 'Places to go, things to do … Oops, sorry, guess I crushed you.'

Modesty is no more popular today than salad is to most five-year-olds, but it's worth the sacrifice, if we can call it one. Most people don't consider it a sacrifice when they take their trash to the garbage can, so if we truly believe we're clearing away rubbish to make room for a blessing in our lives, let's have hearts full of joyful expectation. As we dare to move forward in loving obedience, to dress with grace instead of *disgrace*, we'll find that God changes our hearts and gives us a new perspective on what is beautiful.

We must also carry modesty into our interaction with men, not just into our clothing choices. A modest demeanor is much harder to come by than a modest outfit, though. To possess that treasure, we'll need to spend much time praying, asking God for special strength and wisdom. We'll have to be strict with ourselves—resisting the temptation to flirt, to work our way into men's attention and call out their affections with small-talk, teasing, and joking. We'll need to keep one-on-one conversations with them brief, even about the best of topics (two people talking by themselves creates an intimate feel. That isn't always a good thing.). We should be cheerful and sweet, but with the reserve that makes it clear that we intend to guard guys' hearts, as well as our own, from temptation. We should be courteous, kind, and hospitable, but be sure we're that way to *everyone*: Doing favors as merely a way to send 'like' vibes to someone doesn't count as true service.

We can't afford to lie to ourselves and make the concept of 'brothers and sisters in Christ' a license for doing away with boundaries—the boundaries of purity Christ Himself has given us to keep. The way to show love for our brothers in Christ is to pray for them and make choices that won't make their battle for godly manhood harder than it already is—helping them rise to their full potential as God's sons, instead of being a source of distraction.

Living like this, our hearts may not flutter because we've won first place in the 'Look at me!' contest, but they'll thrill with the joyful satisfaction of a new focus: To love God with every fiber of our being, and to bless others with the time and thought that we used to waste on ourselves.

When we no longer live to be noticed, and are content to be a 'strawberry under the leaves,' we're giving God the job of finding the one to pick us. In His perfect timing, He'll direct a man our way who is patiently listening for Divine directions as he walks through the 'strawberry' patch—not falling for whatever catches his eye first. You see, godly men aren't on the proverbial 'see-food diet.' Like the Biblical character Job, they've made a covenant of purity with their eyes: "I have made a covenant with my eyes; why then should I look (*lustfully*) upon a young woman?" (Job 31:1 NKJV). Instead of bowing to their lusts, they feed on the blessings God gives them as they walk by faith. Patient and lust-overcoming as single men, they're faithful as married men. The girls who marry them needn't fear being tossed to the wayside at the sight of some other 'berry's' charms, once the honeymoon is over and life as usual sets in. After all, commitment and integrity are nothing new to these guys.

Gentlemen:

> "... *Behold, the husbandman waiteth for*
> *the precious fruit of the earth and*
> *hath long patience for it* ... "
> *– James 5:7 KJV*

It's natural, so natural, for you to fall for the exposed strawberries: The girls who dress to catch your carnal eye. It's prevalent, so heart-breakingly prevalent, for you to fall for the exposed strawberries: The girls who aren't God's will, but aren't so hard to find. I know it—the virtuous woman is an endangered species these days. Solomon hit the nail on the head when he said, "One man among a thousand I have found; but a woman among all these I have not found" (Ecclesiastes 7:28 NKJV). Satan is working overtime on us women, because he knows the influence we can have over you—for good or for evil. Only God knows how many lights for the Lord have been dimmed, or even snuffed out, through the influence of an unconsecrated wife!

God is calling you to patience, by His grace to set your sights high, to become men who would rather be alone than with girls whose hearts are wrapped around the fashions and customs of a "planet in rebellion." Please, before you say marriage vows, say singleness vows: Vow to stay single if getting married means settling for anything less than what God has shown you to be right. Don't allow loneliness or attraction to redefine your standards. The people in your life today are not necessarily the ones who'll be in your life tomorrow, so don't settle for what's in plain sight—that person you know who was once out of the question, but is starting to look acceptable in the light of desperation (i.e., 'She's the only one my age at church … I'm getting older, almost into my mid-20's … Wow, I never noticed before how much we have in common: We both like spaghetti and the color blue … '). If you have faith in God's wisdom and provision, they're not your only option.

I just heard a story about a Seventh-Day Adventist young man living in Communist Russia during the 1950's. Labeled "an enemy of the people" for his faith, Mikhail Kulakov endured a five-year sentence in a grueling labor camp. When this period was up, he was "eternally exiled" to Siberia. Talk about a place for a 26-year-old guy to feel hopeless at the thought of finding a wife, and a Seventh-Day-Adventist one at that! As my brother once said of Alaska, the ratio of eligible girls to papaya trees there was equal. But, as Mikhail held onto the faith that persecution had only strengthened, God brought Anna, the love of his life, to him through a miraculous chain of events. Growing up in Siberia, her faith in God's ability to provide had been tested, too. The other girls in her village had married, but still she was alone. One day as she stood at the fence, wistfully watching her neighbor's wedding, her father came up and tenderly encouraged her with the verse, "Seek ye first the kingdom of God, and His righteousness; and all these things shall be added unto you" (Matthew 6:33 KJV). She chose to follow his counsel and was deeply blessed. Mikhail and Anna's over 50 years of happy marriage and loving ministry[5] (thankfully not all spent in Siberia!) illustrate that no circumstance limits the One who has promised us "a future and a hope" (Jeremiah 29:11 NKJV). Whether that future is as singles or marrieds (new term, I guess), it is joyful and beautiful. Don't get the grubby fingerprints of unbelief on it by taking things into your own hands. Wait on Him. Sure, all the men around you may be eating strawberries (probably green ones), but God never feeds His bachelors ramen or fast food. He'll spread a feast of goodness so fulfilling that you won't be on the search for satisfaction (and that means a lot, for my hollow-legged brothers have shown me just what it takes to feed a man). Then, if it's part of His plan, someday He will stand by your side and say, 'My son, there's more out there than what you know and what you see. I want to show you something. Look—this strawberry has been ripening just

---

[5] The whole story can be found in the book, *Though the Heavens Fall*, by Mikhail P. Kulakov.

for you; she's grown sweeter with every passing day. You've been a diligent seeker, always on the quest for a deeper relationship with Me (see Jeremiah 29:13). You've served Me with the strength and energy of your manhood. You've believed Me enough to turn from the mirages that would have been the end of your joy and usefulness, and now I give you this treasure, a blessing that brings 'no sorrow with it' (Proverbs 10:22 KJV).'

Ladies & Gentlemen:

When I first heard the following words a few years ago[6], they left a deep impression on me. Every time I read them, their recalibrating effect is powerful. They inspire me to stop disbelieving God's promises, and instead, to go through with what so many stop short of: To be content to wait on Him and allow His love to fill a void that feels human-shaped.

Believe and Be Satisfied

"Everyone longs to give themselves completely to someone, to have a deep relationship with another, to be loved thoroughly and exclusively. But God says, 'No, not until you're satisfied and fulfilled and content with being loved by Me alone. I love you, My child, and until you discover that only in me is your satisfaction to be found, you will not be capable of

---

[6] Quoted in a sermon by Pastor Keala Thompson entitled, "Finding Your Soul-Mate." His messages are available on www.audioverse.org.

the perfect human relationship that I have planned for you. You will never be united with another until you are united with Me, exclusive of any other desires and longings. I want you to stop planning, stop wishing, and allow Me to give you the most thrilling relationship that exists, one that you can't even imagine. I want you to have the best. Please allow Me to bring it to you. Keep watching Me, expecting the greatest things. Keep experiencing the satisfaction that I am. Keep learning and listening to the things I tell you. Don't be anxious, don't worry, don't look around at the things that others have gotten, or that I have given them. Don't look at the things that you think that you want—just keep looking at Me, or you'll miss what I want to show you. And then, when you are ready, I'll surprise you with a love far more wonderful than you would ever dream. You see, until you are ready, and until the one that I have for you is ready, who I am working with this very minute as I am working with you, so to have both of you ready at the same time, until you're both satisfied exclusively with Me and the life I have prepared for you, you won't be able to experience the love that is based on your relationship with Me. And this is perfect love. And dear one, I want you to have the most wonderful love, I want you to experience a relationship with Me and to enjoy the everlasting beauty, and perfection, and love that I offer. Know that I love you utterly. I am your Heavenly Father. Believe and be satisfied."

– Author Unknown

53

7

The Only Perfume Worth Wearing

"The only way to become selfless is to become Christ-full."
– Anonymous

Artificial fragrances pervade the lives of most people these days, whether it be in the form of soaps, lotions, air fresheners, cleaners, or a favorite perfume or cologne. Our home was no exception, until the Lord led my family and me to the understanding that these supposedly 'good' smells aren't so good for our health. Appealing to our nostrils doesn't necessarily make a chemical safe to inhale! After weeding the offenders from our corner of the world, we've discovered, along with many other benefits, that we have a heightened appreciation for the exquisite natural scents God has infused His creation with. Where I'm taking this probably won't surprise you, but the scent of vine-ripened strawberries is *unsurpassed*. It carries the sweetness of fruit and the perfume of flowers, all in one captivating package. As a berry moves from 'ripe' to 'very ripe,' its fragrance only intensifies, until it is so luscious we could make ourselves light-headed trying to take it all in. Though I recently saw a breakdown of the 42 different plant chemicals present in the smell of a strawberry, exactly how it comes from dirt remains a fascinating mystery. I believe that the Miracle-Worker Who spoke our world into existence in only six days, is still at work, day in and day out.

Love Lesson:

True love has a smell. In the Bible, the book of Ephesians calls it a "savor":

> *"Be ye therefore followers of God, as dear children; and walk in love, as Christ also hath loved us, and hath given himself for us an offering and a sacrifice to God for a sweet-smelling savor. But fornication* (sexual immorality), *and all uncleanness, or covetousness, let it not be once named among you, as becometh saints" (Ephesians 5:1-3 KJV).*

Love smells like unselfishness. It smells like self-sacrifice. It smells like purity and contentment. Any genuinely ripe 'strawberry' will exude these fragrances, and instead of only in the beginning, more and more intensely with the passing of time. When we leave open trays of strawberries in our kitchen overnight, the smell builds and builds until it's so strong that it floats upstairs and greets us when we open our bedroom doors in the morning. Their presence and their ripeness is no secret; everyone in the house catches a whiff. When it comes to relationships, if we think we've found a ripe 'strawberry', maybe we should ask if anyone else can smell anything—everyone 'in the house', or in that person's sphere of influence, ought to be able to testify that our noses aren't playing tricks on us. Do they treat their family with tenderness and commitment, or do they show ingratitude for all that has been invested in them by being disloyal and selfish? Do people of all ages and interests find a listening ear and a caring heart in them, or do they act brain-dead and introverted until they've escaped to their favorite clique? What about the elderly: Do they 'smell' the wonderful character you think you do, or are they made to feel that their value has faded alongside their youthfulness?

We all fall short of who we should be. And qualifying as 'marriage-material' is the least of it. Every human being has been called to pervade the world with the fragrance of God's righteousness. Sadly, we naturally pollute the atmosphere around us with the toxic smog of self-centeredness. We hurt our fellow humans, and leave all Heaven sorrowfully disappointed in us. Try as we might to change, we are unable to draw the sweet smell of unselfish love from the soil of our hearts. But if we come to our Creator-Redeemer, He will perform the miracle of grace that leaves those around us wondering at how such Christ-like fragrance can come from the mere dust that we are.

> *"To love as Christ loved means that we must practice self-control. It means that we must show unselfishness at all times and in all places. It means that we must scatter round us kind words and pleasant looks. These cost the giver nothing, but they leave behind a precious fragrance. Their influence for good cannot be estimated. Not only to the receiver, but to the giver, they are a blessing; for they react upon him. Genuine love is a precious attribute of heavenly origin, which increases in fragrance in proportion as it is dispensed to others…"*
>
> *– Our Father Cares, pp. 44, 45*

8

Let Strawberries Be Thy Medicine

*"God gives His best to those who
leave the choice with Him."*
— J. Hudson Taylor, 19th-century missionary to China

Children (and adults, too) look forward to the candy they get at Halloween, but end up sick and enriching the dentist because of all the sugar. They look forward to Christmas because of all the presents, but are miserable afterward as they experience let-down, and squabble with their siblings over their latest, greatest possessions. People like to eat whatever and whenever they want, but then it catches up to them in the form of disease. That's how so many supposed 'pleasures' are: Enjoy now, suffer later. Not so with the gifts of our Heavenly Father: They bring lasting enjoyment and vibrant health (physically and spiritually) to those who receive them.

I'm happy to say that strawberries fit into the "God's gifts" category. We've already established that they're enjoyable. Now what about the health part? Good news! As is the case with all the fruits, vegetables, grains, nuts, seeds, and beans God designed to be man's diet, strawberries are power-packed with nutrition. Wikipedia tells us that the strawberry is "an excellent source of vitamin C, a good source of manganese, and provides several other vitamins and dietary minerals in lesser amounts."[7] Exactly how strawberries affect our health is a little-researched topic, but the studies that have been done reveal that we don't have to wait for research to know that God's food is good: Strawberries decrease the risk of heart-disease, contain anti-inflammatory and anti-cancer phytochemicals, and bring LDL and total cholesterol down. Experiments also suggest that they assist the body in ridding itself of arsenic. I guess the ancient Romans were onto something when they used them for medicine!

Love Lesson:

What do we say when a person is in a relationship with someone who has a bad influence on them? "So and so is not 'good for' him/her." They may think they've found something delicious, but it's deficient and tainted by 'pesticides' and 'GMO's' ('Good Marriage Obstructions'). Any 'strawberry' worth having—someone who is God's gift to us—will always come with health benefits. When

---

[7] Wikipedia

we "send them in" to the test-lab of prayer, godly counsel, and time, the following tests will reveal 'nutritional' levels that are no cause for shame:

- Is he/she an excellent source of encouragement, kindness, and friendship?
- Will I be inspired to be more earnest and sincere in the things of God, or will there be a constant undercurrent attempting to sweep me into indifference and hardness of heart?
- Will we have an anti-inflammatory influence on each other, or will issues and arguments be our 'daily bread'?
- Will our love annihilate the conditions that breed the cancers of bitterness and unfaithfulness?
- Will we help each other become purer, or will we poison each other with character traits that have never been yielded to God?

No doubt, a person with a character that answers all these questions in the positive is a rare find. Like we discussed in the "Gentlemen" section of Chapter 6, though, settling for lesser quality is *never* an option! The story of Abraham warns us what happens when, in the face of impossibilities, we try to get *God's* blessings *our* way (see Genesis 16 & 21). Do we want our lives embittered by our own versions of Hagar and Ishmael? "Faith and patience" (Hebrews 6:12 KJV), not our own fear-based schemes, are what it takes to receive God's promises.

George Muller, a man with faith and patience like few have ever dared to exercise, once stated,

> *"Faith does not operate in the realm of the possible. There is no glory for God in that which is humanly possible. Faith begins where man's power ends."*

If finding a godly companion seems to be in the realm of the impossible for us, we should be grateful. That way, if it ever happens, we'll know it was God's doing—the only thing we ought to be interested in, anyway. Marriage is only worth it if it's "what God hath joined together" (Matthew 19:6 KJV). Notice that word "joined." It's active, not passive. If marriage is on God's agenda for any one of us, it's a project He's actively working on, not something He's left us to figure out. We can let go of our 'strawberry stress' and be at peace, conscious that the precious oneness we so much desire is a gift only He can handcraft. Without His touch, a wedding is nothing more than the kick-off of a mockery—a union that exists on a certificate alone.

The Creator of heaven and earth has lost none of His creativity. He still designs and breathes wonders into existence. If only we'd give Him permission to do so in our personal worlds! He won't force His services on us. After all, He's a gentleman.

Love At Home

There is beauty all around, when there's love at home;
There is joy in every sound, when there's love at home.
Peace and plenty here abide, smiling fair on every side;
Time doth softly, sweetly glide, when there's love at home.

Chorus: Love at home, love at home;
Time doth softly, sweetly glide when there's love at home.

In the cottage there is joy, when there's love at home;
Hate and envy ne'er annoy, when there's love at home.
Roses blossom 'neath our feet, all the earth's a garden sweet,
Making life a bliss complete, when there's love at home.

Kindly heaven smiles above, when there's love at home;
All the earth is filled with love, when there's love at home.
Sweeter sings the brooklet by, brighter beams the azure sky;
O, there's One who smiles on high when there's love at home.

Jesus, make me wholly Thine, then there's love at home;
May Thy sacrifice be mine, then there's love at home.
Safely from all harm I'll rest, with no sinful care distressed,
Through Thy tender mercy blessed, when there's love at home.

– J. H. McNaughton[8]

---

[8] A hymn published in the early Adventist hymnal, *Christ in Song*.
It can also be found in the newer *Seventh-Day Adventist Hymnal*
(#652), but the second verse was left out.

9

Two Stems: "The End"?

*"Neither death, nor life ... shall be able to
separate us from the love of God ... "*
– Romans 8:38,39 KJV

According to 'studies' (me observing people as they eat),
the average life-span of a vine-ripened strawberry is five
seconds: Chomp, chomp, chomp, swallow. After that, a
stem and some good memories are all that's left. That's
how all the joys of this life are: Sweet, but temporary. Even
the ripest 'strawberries'—the happiest, most beautiful
marriages—face the pain of separation, not because love
has died, but because *we* die. Our lives are only a blink
in time. But is a 'stem'—the gloom of life all-gone—the
only thing we have to anticipate in the long run, as we let
go of fear and allow the 'strawberry' to ripen? I'm grateful
the answer is 'No.' To learn to trust while in the 'berry
patch' is to build something eternal: A relationship with
the *Creator* of the strawberry. Knowing Him here and

now is but the beginning of a bright future with Him and with each other that will stretch beyond the limits of time. The grave may press 'pause' on life, but He has promised to restore it to all those who died wanting to taste still more of His love.

The more I think over each strawberry lesson I've shared in this book, the more it sinks in that connecting with this love is what lies at the heart of each one. Without finding that connection, we come away with nothing more than a cute new code word for a potential spouse. I hope that the following key points, running like a thread through every page, have made a lasting impression:

1. Waiting instead of dating is about *believing in* God's love.

When it comes to God, every human has to weigh the evidence and decide on one of two beliefs: "He loves me," or, "He loves me not." As I shared in Chapter 1, the picture of God I get through the Bible has settled it for me: I believe that He loves me, and not only that He loves me, but that He *is* Love Itself (see 1 John 4:8).

Anyone who truly believes that God is love will prove it with their choices. Instead of begrudging Him even the bare minimum, they'll want Him to be involved in every detail of their life, because there's nothing that isn't made better by love. And I believe they'll especially crave His involvement in their love-life, because "love" without *Love* is no love at all.

2. Waiting instead of dating is about *experiencing* God's love.

We each have our own idea of what love is and how to find it. But the human heart isn't safe to follow—we often pursue the bitterest curses of our lives, all the while thinking we're chasing our heart's desire. God sees our every disappointment, our every heart-break, and longs to give us something better: His kind of love. True love. Love that is found by following Him, not our hearts. As we dare to turn our backs on what's natural and listen to what He says instead, life becomes a table spread with His goodness. And sometimes He serves 'strawberries' for dessert … Ripe ones …

3. Waiting instead of dating is about *revealing* God's love.

The home was meant to be a foretaste of Heaven, a loom where the traits of husband and wife are woven together to reveal what God is like. But sin has made it a place of brokenness. More often than not, "family" means being bound to abuse and pain. God needs people who will come to Him for the power to defy their genes, break cycles of dysfunction, and, once again, make marriage and family a reflection of His love. What could bring this about more painlessly than starting out right—us picking and being ripe 'strawberries'? God specializes in transforming the worst of situations, but "an ounce of prevention is worth a pound of cure." By the way, here's a bonus strawberry lesson: Only seeds from *ripe* fruit will sprout well. If we want our "seed" (see Malachi 2:15)— our children—to be men and women of spiritual power, we need to, once again, avoid the green and wait for the "*daaark*" red 'strawberries.'

Final Thought:

We all have our dreams, but none of us know what tomorrow really holds. Life is uncertain, and we live in trouble-filled times. As we face the future, let's get and keep our focus right: The point of life is not 'Prepare to meet your husband or wife.' The Bible tells us what it really is: "Prepare to meet thy God" (Amos 4:12 KJV)). For those who do this, the only happily-ever-after love-experience that exists is waiting: Eternity with our Creator and Savior, Jesus.

Recommended Reading:

I'm thankful for the privilege of growing up with an abundance of good books. Books are powerful tools that shape our thinking, and therefore, our characters. That is, if we read them ... Many people are so stuffed with entertainment and technology that they have no room for this wholesome pastime. The fact that you're on the final pages of this book (Great job! You ate the *whole* sandwich—even the crusts!) tells me that you don't fit into this category—your appetite is still good. Here are just some of the titles that have impacted me, and that I recommend you get your hands on:

- *I Kissed Dating Goodbye* by Joshua Harris.
  More on the waiting vs. dating topic!

- *Not Even A Hint* by Joshua Harris.
  How to trade lust for true love and satisfaction.

- *Steps to Christ* by Ellen White.
  Rubber-meets-the-road instruction on how to establish a steady, beautiful relationship with Jesus.

(Continued on the next page.)

- *The Great Controversy* by Ellen White.
  If you're a history-brain, you'll love this one! It recounts events from A.D. 70 all the way to the late 1800's, and tackles mysteries of the future such as the Mark of the Beast and the Antichrist. It also answers many questions about God that keep us from being able to view Him as a Being of love. For example, how can He burn people in Hell forever? …

- *Operation Blueprint: Earth's Final Movie* by Ivor Meyers.
  Find out what the ancient Hebrew tent-temple has to do with you and me today.

I Long to See Jesus

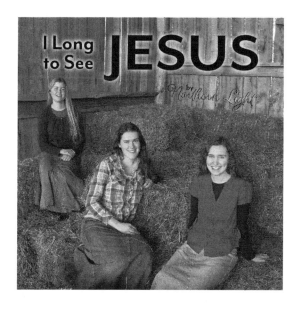

Go to store.cdbaby.com to order your copy of "I Long to See Jesus", Savanna and her sisters' first music album. It is also available in MP3 format on amazon.com. Each original song, accented by guitar, piano, and alto recorder, will comfort and encourage you on the journey toward perfect trust and the joys of obedience.